Editor

Mary S. Jones, M.A.

Cover Artist

Tony Carillo

Managing Editor

Ina Massler Levin, M.A.

Creative Director

Karen J. Goldfluss, M.S. Ed.

Art Production Manager

Kevin Barnes

Imaging

Nathan P. Rivera

Publisher

Mary D. Smith, M.S. Ed.

Author

Debbie Connolly, M.A.

Teacher Created Resources, Inc.

6421 Industry Way

Westminster, CA 92683

www.teachercreated.com

ISBN: 978-1-4206-8774-3

© *2007 Teacher Created Resources, Inc.*

Made in U.S.A.

Table of Contents

Introduction

About the Activities

Classroom teachers have, in one form or another, used the many spelling activities included in this book for several years. The author has personally put them into practice in her classroom for over 20 years and has seen the successful outcomes. The activities came about in the early 1980s when individualized teaching was all the rage. At that time, most of the spelling activities that came with spelling programs did not provide enough practice. These activities were developed to enrich the "weekly spelling list." They have been used since then in many different contexts.

The activities fit perfectly with any language arts program and also with a whole language approach, where students are given a spelling focus or rule, they generate a list, decide on their spelling focus or rule, and are tested by a partner. The activities fit any venue in use. The aspect the students will enjoy most is the element of choice. The activities work well for students with different learning styles.

Using the Spelling Contracts

The contracts are easy to use. Simply copy the contract that you would like students to use, draw a star next to the activity or activities that students must complete, and write the number of other activities that they must complete on the line. Of the remaining activities, students can choose which activities they would like to complete. Students also need a copy of the Word List (page 9) along with the Contract Cover Sheet (page 8), where students will write the titles of their chosen activities and where you will write their scores. (See samples on pages 5–7.) Included is a Blank Contract (page 18) where new activities or arrangements of activities of your choosing can be made.

Write the spelling words and the corresponding spelling focus or rule on the Word List, then reproduce for your students. The support activities may be handled in several ways. The suggested way to set up the activities is in a file cabinet with a folder for each activity. When students decide which activities they will be doing, they simply go to the file cabinet and grab the activities that they need. There are many other ways that the activities can be organized for your students. It will depend on your situation and your preferences.

Sample Spelling Contract

SPELLING

Complete the starred (★) activity or activities first, then choose __2__ more to complete. Place a check in the box indicating which activities you chose. Staple all work together, including this contract page, your word list, and cover sheet.

Sort your words by syllables.	Write a paragraph using as many of your words as you can. It must make sense. Don't forget a topic sentence!	Make a word wheel with eight of the words you are having the most difficulty learning on the outside circle and their definitions on the inside.
(Syllable Sort, page 19) ☐	(Paragraph, page 20) ☑	(Word Wheel, pages 21–23) ☐
Write your words three times each in cursive. ★	"Shape spell" each of your words. Then, go back and fill in the shapes using your list.	Write your words in alphabetical order.
(Three Times in Cursive, page 24) ☑	(Shape Spelling, page 25) ☐	(Alphabetical Order, page 26) ☑
Scramble your words. Then, go back and unscramble them without looking at your list.	Look up your words in a dictionary. Write the pronunciation and part of speech.	Complete spelling book pages _79 and 80_. ★
(Scramble Words, page 27) ☐	(Dictionary Challenge, page 28) ☐	☑

Introduction

Using the Spelling Contracts *(cont.)*

These spelling activities work great for homework assignments. The contracts are recommended to be completed in one week. Assign them on Monday and have students take them home for the week and turn them in on Friday. Everything (Contract Cover Sheet, Word List, Contract, and activities) should be stapled together before the assignment is handed in.

Note that on all of the contracts there is an activity that states, "Complete spelling book pages _____." This can be used with the support materials from any spelling or language arts program you may have in your classroom. Most language arts series have worksheet activities that help students practice the week's focus or rule. Simply run these off and have students staple them to the contract with their other work. If you don't have any other program to follow, disregard this activity or white it out and write in a new activity before reproducing the page for students.

Where to Get the Spelling Words

If you are not using a spelling or language arts series that provides a weekly list and spelling focus, here are a few other options. Using books such as The *Reading Teacher's Book of Lists* by Dr. Edward Fry, you can generate lists using a certain focus. You can also do an online search for weekly spelling lists categorized by grade. One other suggestion is to choose a spelling focus, use that as a mini lesson, and then have students look through their independent reading books or in classroom textbooks to generate words that fit the focus. In a brainstorm, write all words found on a large classroom chart and choose the words for the week's list from those generated by the students. For example, if the focus was making words plural by adding *–es*, all of the words generated would fit that focus (*couches, watches, wishes*, etc.).

Suggestions for Grading

When grading the contracts, have a set criterion. For instance, in order to earn a satisfactory grade (passing), students must complete a minimum of four activities. To exceed, they would do all of the activities. Notice that each contract states, "Complete the starred (☆) activity or activities first, then choose ____ more to complete." The teacher decides the minimum criteria and writes the number of activities to be completed. (Remember to star the activities you deem mandatory.) Having the flexibility to choose the number of required activities helps for those short school weeks. Change the criteria to fit the time constraints. Write students' scores on the Contract Cover Sheet.

Sample Word List

Spelling Focus: words that end in -ch and -sh

1. _____ match
2. _____ watch
3. _____ catch
4. _____ torch
5. _____ touch
6. _____ scratch
7. _____ lunch
8. _____ bench
9. _____ punch
10. _____ hunch

11. _____ dish
12. _____ wash
13. _____ splash
14. _____ radish
15. _____ push
16. _____ fish
17. _____ crush
18. _____ wish
19. _____ push
20. _____ hush

Bonus Word(s):

1. _____ surprisingly

2. _____ misunderstand

SPELLING

Complete the starred (⭐) activity or activities first, then choose __2__ more to complete. Place a check in the box indicating which activities you chose. Staple all work together, including this contract page, your word list, and cover sheet.

Sort your words by syllables. (Syllable Sort, page 19) ☐	Write a paragraph using as many of your words as you can. It must make sense. Don't forget a topic sentence! (Paragraph, page 20) ☑	Make a word wheel with eight of the words you are having the most difficulty learning on the outside circle and their definitions on the inside. (Word Wheel, pages 21–23) ☐
Write your words three times each in cursive. ⭐ (Three Times in Cursive, page 24) ☑	"Shape spell" each of your words. Then, go back and fill in the shapes using your list. (Shape Spelling, page 25) ☐	Write your words in alphabetical order. (Alphabetical Order, page 26) ☑
Scramble your words. Then, go back and unscramble them without looking at your list. (Scramble Words, page 27) ☐	Look up your words in a dictionary. Write the pronunciation and part of speech. (Dictionary Challenge, page 28) ☐	Complete spelling book pages *79 and 80*. ⭐ ☑

Sample Contract Cover Sheet

Name: _____ Mary Jones _____ **Final Score:** _____

Directions: List the activities you have completed below. Staple this page to the top of your contract, word list, and activities you have completed.

	Activity	**Score**
1.	Spelling book pages 79 and 80	
2.	Three Times in Cursive	
3.	Paragraph	
4.	Alphabetical Order	
5.		
6.		
7.		
8.		
9.		

Contract Cover Sheet

Name: _____   **Final Score:** _____

Directions: List the activities you have completed below. Staple this page to the top of your contract, word list, and activities you have completed.

Activity   **Score**

1. _____   _____

2. _____   _____

3. _____   _____

4. _____   _____

5. _____   _____

6. _____   _____

7. _____   _____

8. _____   _____

9. _____   _____

Word List

Spelling Focus: _____

1. _____   11. _____

2. _____   12. _____

3. _____   13. _____

4. _____   14. _____

5. _____   15. _____

6. _____   16. _____

7. _____   17. _____

8. _____   18. _____

9. _____   19. _____

10. _____   20. _____

Bonus Word(s):

1. _____   2. _____

SPELLING

Use with any word list.

Complete the starred (☆) activity or activities first, then choose _____ more to complete. Place a check in the box indicating which activities you chose. Staple all work together, including this contract page, your word list, and cover sheet.

Sort your words by syllables. (Syllable Sort, page 19) ☐	Write a paragraph using as many of your words as you can. It must make sense. Don't forget a topic sentence! (Paragraph, page 20) ☐	Make a word wheel with eight of the words you are having the most difficulty learning on the outside circle and their definitions on the inside. (Word Wheel, pages 21–23) ☐
Write your words three times each in cursive. (Three Times in Cursive, page 24) ☐	"Shape spell" each of your words. Then, go back and fill in the shapes using your list. (Shape Spelling, page 25) ☐	Write your words in alphabetical order. (Alphabetical Order, page 26) ☐
Scramble your words. Then, go back and unscramble them without looking at your list. (Scramble Words, page 27) ☐	Look up your words in a dictionary. Write the pronunciation and part of speech. (Dictionary Challenge, page 28) ☐	Complete spelling book pages _____. ☐

SPELLING

Use with any word list.

Complete the starred (☆) activity or activities first, then choose _____ more to complete. Place a check in the box indicating which activities you chose. Staple all work together, including this contract page, your word list, and cover sheet.

Make a flip book using eight of your most difficult words. Write words and definitions on the top flap and use each word in an original sentence underneath. (Flip Book, page 29) ☐	Have someone give you a spelling test and correct it. Write any misspelled words five times each on the back. (Spelling Test, page 30) ☐	Create a word search using your word list. (Word Search, page 31) ☐
Write each of your list words. Using a thesaurus, find a synonym or an antonym and write a sentence using the new word. (Thesaurus Sentences, pages 32–33) ☐	Write each of your words (use grid paper, one letter per square), cut them apart, and rebuild them using the letters. Glue your words back together. (Spelling Scramble, pages 34–35) ☐	Make a list of other words that fit your spelling focus of the week. How many words can you find? (Spelling Focus, page 36) ☐
Speed spell your words three times each — fast! (Speed Spell, page 37) ☐	Type your word list on the computer using an interesting font. Print and attach to the contract. ☐	Complete spelling book pages _____. ☐

SPELLING

Use with any word list.

Complete the starred (☆) activity or activities first, then choose ____ more to complete. Place a check in the box indicating which activities you chose. Staple all work together, including this contract page, your word list, and cover sheet.

Make a word chain using at least five of your words. How long can you make your chain? (Word Chains, pages 38–39) ☐	Write your words in column one, copy them to column two, fold and write from memory to column three. Unfold to check your work. (Column Spelling, page 40) ☐	Find your spelling words in a dictionary and write the two guide words you find at the top of each page. (Guide Words, page 41) ☐
Write your words three times each using a different color each time. (Three Times in Color, page 42) ☐	Write a short story using as many words as you can. Underline the words you used. (Short Story, page 43) ☐	Write sentences using your spelling words but replace your spelling words with a blank space. Give them to a friend to fill in the correct spelling word. (Fill in the Blank, pages 44–45) ☐
Go Fish! Make pairs of cards for each of your words. Play a matching game with a partner. Attach the cards in a resealable bag to the contract. ☐	Complete spelling book pages _____ . ☐	☐

SPELLING

Use with any word list.

Complete the starred (☆) activity or activities first, then choose _____ more to complete. Place a check in the box indicating which activities you chose. Staple all work together, including this contract page, your word list, and cover sheet.

Create a crossword puzzle using your words' definitions as clues. (Crossword Puzzle, pages 46–47) ☐	Sort your words into categories of your own choosing. Write the category at the top of each column. (Word Sort, page 48) ☐	Write your words in sentences using alliteration. (Alliteration, page 49) ☐
Look up your words in a dictionary and write their definitions. (Dictionary Definitions, pages 50–51) ☐	In one column, write 10 of the words from your list that you are having the most problem with. In the second column, write their definitions out of order. Trade papers with a partner and match the words to their definitions. (Word Match, page 52) ☐	Using three sets of 10 cards, write the names of people or types of animals, past tense verbs, and things (one per card). Pick one card from each pile and write silly sentences. (Who Did What?, pages 53–55) ☐
Make pairs of cards for each of your words. Play a game of concentration. Attach the cards in a resealable bag to the contract. ☐	Make a set of flashcards with your words. Practice spelling each word quietly to yourself. Attach the cards in a resealable bag to the contract. ☐	Complete spelling book pages _____. ☐

SPELLING

Use with words containing prefixes and suffixes.

Complete the starred (★) activity or activities first, then choose ____ more to complete. Place a check in the box indicating which activities you chose. Staple all work together, including this contract page, your word list, and cover sheet.

Have someone give you a spelling test and correct it. Write any misspelled words five times each on the back. (Spelling Test, page 30) ☐	Sort your words into categories of your own choosing. Write the category names at the top of the columns. (Word Sort, page 48) ☐	Separate your base or root word from your prefix/suffix. How did the word part change the meaning of your root word? (Prefix/Suffix, page 56) ☐
Make a list of other words that use the same prefixes/suffixes as your list words. ☐	In one column, write your spelling words in ABC order. In a second column, write their root words in ABC order. ☐	Use a dictionary to look up your prefixes/ suffixes. What do they mean and how do they change a root word? ☐
Complete spelling book pages _____. ☐	☐	☐

SPELLING

Use with a word list of contractions.

Complete the starred (★) activity or activities first, then choose _____ more to complete. Place a check in the box indicating which activities you chose. Staple all work together, including this contract page, your word list, and cover sheet.

Make a flip book using eight of your contractions. On the top flap, write the two words that make up each contraction. Write the contraction underneath. (Flip Book, page 29) ☐	Have someone give you a spelling test and correct it. Write any misspelled words five times each on the back. (Spelling Test, page 30) ☐	Write your contractions and list the two words that make up each word. Then write the letters that were left out. (Contraction Parts, page 57) ☐
Make a list of contractions. Write as many as you can find. Write the contraction and the two words that make it up on each line. (Contraction List, page 58) ☐	Go Fish! Make cards for your contractions. On one card write your word. On another, write the two words that make-up the contraction. Play a matching game with a partner. Attach the cards in a resealable bag to the contract. ☐	Concentration Game: Make a pair of cards for each word and play concentration. Attach the cards in a resealable bag to the contract. ☐
Make a set of flashcards with your words. Practice spelling each word quietly to yourself. Attach the cards in a resealable bag to the contract. ☐	Complete spelling book pages _____. ☐	☐

SPELLING

Use with a word list of homophones.

Complete the starred (☆) activity or activities first, then choose _____ more to complete. Place a check in the box indicating which activities you chose. Staple all work together, including this contract page, your word list, and cover sheet.

Make a word wheel. Write eight of your homophones on the outer circle and their pairs under the flaps. (Word Wheel, pages 21–23) ☐	Write your words in cursive three times each. (Three Times in Cursive, page 24) ☐	Make a flip book with eight of your homophones on the top flaps and their pairs underneath. (Flip Book, page 29) ☐
Have someone give you a spelling test and correct it. Write any misspelled words five times each on the back. (Spelling Test, page 30) ☐	Write each of your words. Using a thesaurus, find a synonym or antonym for each and write sentences using the new words. (Thesaurus Sentences, pages 32–33) ☐	Write sentences using both of your homophones. Leave spaces where they would go. Trade papers with a partner and complete each other's sentences. (Blank Homophone Sentences, pages 59–60) ☐
Write sentences using both of your homophones. (Homophone Sentences, pages 61–62) ☐	Make a list of other homophone pairs. (Homophone List, page 63) ☐	Complete spelling book pages _____. ☐

SPELLING

Use with a word list of plurals.

Complete the starred (☆) activity or activities first, then choose ـــــــ more to complete. Place a check in the box indicating which activities you chose. Staple all work together, including this contract page, your word list, and cover sheet.

Make a word wheel using eight of your words. Write the singular form on the outside circle and the plural form under the flap. (Word Wheel, pages 21–23) ☐	Write your words in cursive three times each. (Three Times in Cursive, page 24) ☐	Make a flip book using eight of your words. The top flap should be the singular form of each word and the plural form should be underneath. (Flip Book, page 29) ☐
Have someone give you a spelling test and correct it. Write any misspelled words five times each on the back. (Spelling Test, page 30) ☐	Make a crossword puzzle with your words. The clues should be the singular forms. (Crossword Puzzle, pages 46–47) ☐	Write your list of plurals in one column, and then write them as singular in the next. (Singulars and Plurals, page 64) ☐
Sort your words according to how they are made into plurals. Then find other words that fit that rule. ☐	Make a concentration game and play it. On one card write the singular form and on the other write the plural form. Attach the cards in a resealable bag to the contract. ☐	Complete spelling book pages _____ . ☐

SPELLING

Complete the starred (☆) activity or activities first, then choose _____ more to complete. Place a check in the box indicating which activities you chose. Staple all work together, including this contract page, your word list, and cover sheet.

☐	☐	☐
☐	☐	☐
☐	☐	☐

Syllable Sort

Sort your word list by the number of syllables you hear in each word. Place each word in the correct column.

ONE OR TWO SYLLABLES (label how many)	THREE SYLLABLES	FOUR OR MORE SYLLABLES (label how many)

Paragraph

Write a paragraph using as many words from your word list as you can. The paragraph must make sense. Underline your topic sentence and number the supporting details. Write the words you use in the box below.

Word Wheel

Cut out both parts of the word wheel (pages 22–23). Assemble using a brad at the center. Remember to line up the arrow with the middle of the word space before you write under the flap. The spelling word that the arrow points to needs to correlate with the writing under the flap that is across from it. Check your contract for specific activity instructions.

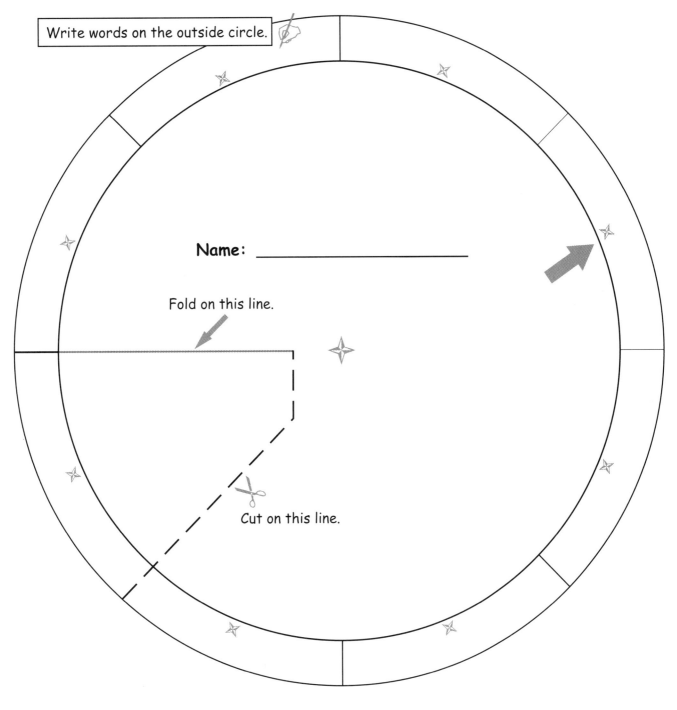

Write words on the outside circle.

Name: _____

Fold on this line.

Cut on this line.

Word Wheel

Cut out the circle below. Attach it on top of the bigger circle (page 23) using a brad at the center. Cut along the dashed line and fold along the gray line.

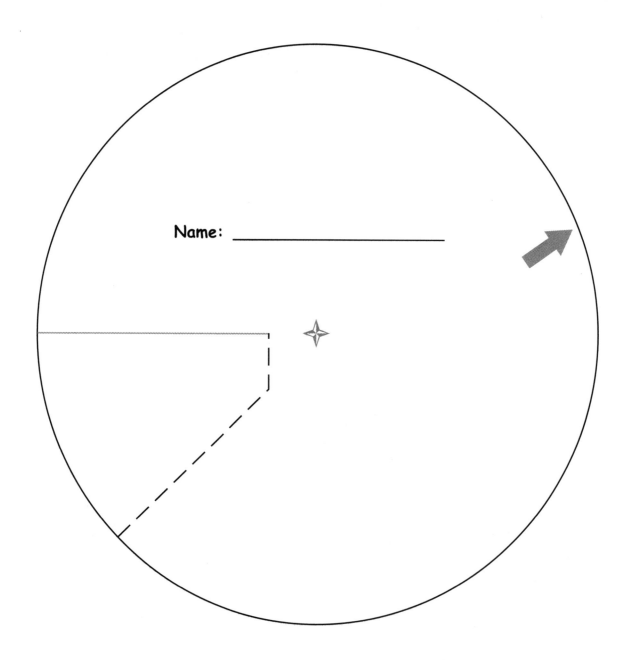

Name: _____

Word Wheel

Cut along the outer circle below. Attach it underneath the smaller circle (page 22) using a brad at the center. Write spelling words in the outer circle.

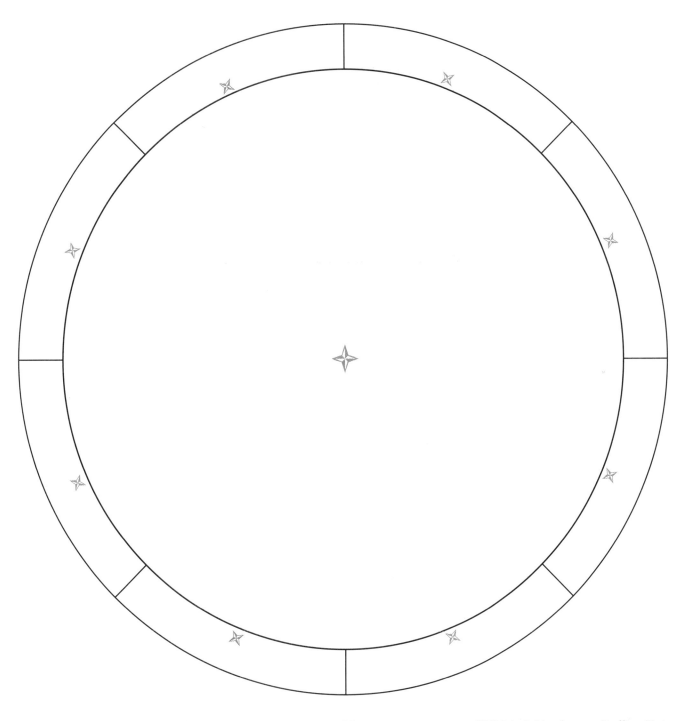

Three Times in Cursive

Using your best handwriting, write each word three times each. On your third try, write it without looking at your list. Check to make sure you spelled it correctly.

1. _____   _____   _____

2. _____   _____   _____

3. _____   _____   _____

4. _____   _____   _____

5. _____   _____   _____

6. _____   _____   _____

7. _____   _____   _____

8. _____   _____   _____

9. _____   _____   _____

10. _____   _____   _____

11. _____   _____   _____

12. _____   _____   _____

13. _____   _____   _____

14. _____   _____   _____

15. _____   _____   _____

16. _____   _____   _____

17. _____   _____   _____

18. _____   _____   _____

19. _____   _____   _____

20. _____   _____   _____

Bonus Word(s):

1. _____   _____   _____

2. _____   _____   _____

Shape Spelling

Shape spelling is a visual way of practicing your words. Choose a word from your list (don't go in order) and draw the shape boxes without letters. When you are done, use your word list and fill each box with the letters that make up the words.

Example: Below are the shape boxes for the word *huge*: one tall letter (h), one short letter (u), one hanging letter (g), and one short letter (e).

huge

Alphabetical Order

Write your words in alphabetical order. Don't forget any bonus words.

1. _____

2. _____

3. _____

4. _____

5. _____

6. _____

7. _____

8. _____

9. _____

10. _____

11. _____

12. _____

13. _____

14. _____

15. _____

16. _____

17. _____

18. _____

19. _____

20. _____

21. _____

22. _____

26

Scramble Words

In the left column, scramble your words in random order (don't scramble them in order).
In the right column, unscramble the words without using your word list. Don't forget any
bonus words.

Scrambled Words   **Unscrambled Words**

_____   _____

_____   _____

_____   _____

_____   _____

_____   _____

_____   _____

_____   _____

_____   _____

_____   _____

_____   _____

_____   _____

_____   _____

_____   _____

_____   _____

_____   _____

_____   _____

_____   _____

_____   _____

Dictionary Challenge

Write your spelling word in the first column. Then, look it up in a dictionary. Write the pronunciation (re-spelling) of the word in the second column, and the part of speech in the third column. **Example:** sneeze / snEz / verb

Spelling Word	Pronounciation	Part of Speech
1. _____	_____	_____
2. _____	_____	_____
3. _____	_____	_____
4. _____	_____	_____
5. _____	_____	_____
6. _____	_____	_____
7. _____	_____	_____
8. _____	_____	_____
9. _____	_____	_____
10. _____	_____	_____
11. _____	_____	_____
12. _____	_____	_____
13. _____	_____	_____
14. _____	_____	_____
15. _____	_____	_____
16. _____	_____	_____
17. _____	_____	_____
18. _____	_____	_____
19. _____	_____	_____
20. _____	_____	_____

Bonus Word(s):

1. _____	_____	
2. _____	_____	

Flip Book

Directions: Take an 18" x 9" piece of paper. Fold it lengthwise (hot dog way). Now fold in half. Repeat folding in half two more times. Open your paper to the original fold and you should have eight sections. Now open the paper completely and cut up the folds to the center line on one side only. When you refold, you will have a flip book with eight flaps. Check your contract for specific activity instructions.

Step 1:

Fold lengthwise.

Step 2:

Fold in half three times.

Step 3:

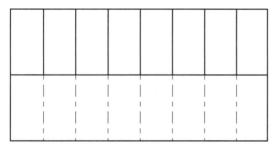

Open up and cut to center line on one half.

Step 4:

Write your words on the outside flaps. Lift flaps to write underneath.

Spelling Test

Have someone give you a spelling test and correct it. Write any misspelled words correctly on the lines next to the words. Then turn your paper over and write any misspelled words five times each on the back.

Test	Corrected Words
1. _____	_____
2. _____	_____
3. _____	_____
4. _____	_____
5. _____	_____
6. _____	_____
7. _____	_____
8. _____	_____
9. _____	_____
10. _____	_____
11. _____	_____
12. _____	_____
13. _____	_____
14. _____	_____
15. _____	_____
16. _____	_____
17. _____	_____
18. _____	_____
19. _____	_____
20. _____	_____

Bonus Word(s):

1. _____   _____

2. _____   _____

Word Search

Make a word search using as many of your list words as you can. You may write them forward, backwards, or diagonally. Then fill in all of the empty boxes with various letters. Now go back and see if you can find all of your words.

1. _____
2. _____
3. _____
4. _____
5. _____
6. _____
7. _____
8. _____

9. _____
10. _____
11. _____
12. _____
13. _____
14. _____
15. _____
16. _____

17. _____
18. _____
19. _____
20. _____

Bonus Word(s):

1. _____
2. _____

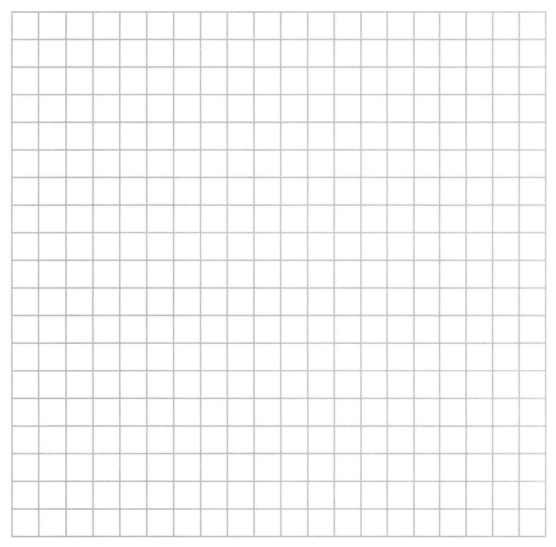

Thesaurus Sentences

Look up your words in the thesaurus and write either a synonym or an antonym for each. Then write a sentence using the synonym or antonym.

Synonym Example: look / stare / I began to <u>stare</u> at the moon.

Word / Synonym or Antonym / Sentence

1. _____
   _____

2. _____
   _____

3. _____
   _____

4. _____
   _____

5. _____
   _____

6. _____
   _____

7. _____
   _____

8. _____
   _____

9. _____
   _____

10. _____
   _____

Thesaurus Sentences

11. _____
    _____

12. _____
    _____

13. _____
    _____

14. _____
    _____

15. _____
    _____

16. _____
    _____

17. _____
    _____

18. _____
    _____

19. _____
    _____

20. _____
    _____

Bonus Word(s):

1. _____
   _____

2. _____
   _____

Spelling Scramble

Write each of your spelling words (one letter per space) using the grid paper on page 35.
Cut apart your words and rebuild them. Glue them onto this page.

1. _____

2. _____

3. _____

4. _____

5. _____

6. _____

7. _____

8. _____

9. _____

10. _____

11. _____

12. _____

13. _____

14. _____

15. _____

16. _____

17. _____

18. _____

19. _____

20. _____

Bonus Word(s):

1. _____

2. _____

Spelling Scramble

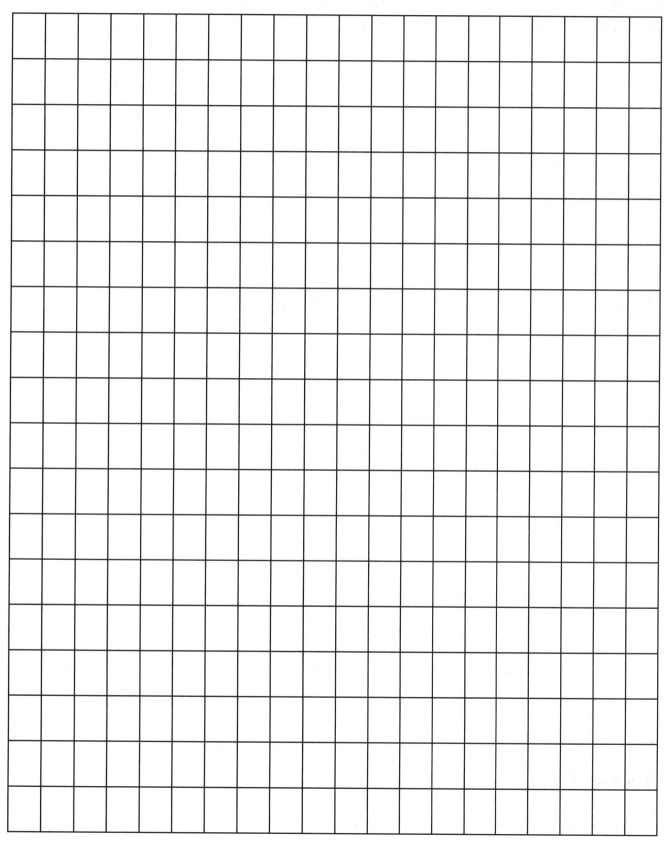

Spelling Focus

Make a list of words that fits your spelling focus or rule. How many words can you find?

Spelling Focus or Rule: _____

_____   _____

_____   _____

_____   _____

_____   _____

_____   _____

_____   _____

_____   _____

_____   _____

Speed Spell

Writing as quickly as you can, speed spell your words three times each. Make sure they are neat.

1. _____   _____   _____

2. _____   _____   _____

3. _____   _____   _____

4. _____   _____   _____

5. _____   _____   _____

6. _____   _____   _____

7. _____   _____   _____

8. _____   _____   _____

9. _____   _____   _____

10. _____   _____   _____

11. _____   _____   _____

12. _____   _____   _____

13. _____   _____   _____

14. _____   _____   _____

15. _____   _____   _____

16. _____   _____   _____

17. _____   _____   _____

18. _____   _____   _____

19. _____   _____   _____

20. _____   _____   _____

Bonus Word(s):

1. _____   _____   _____

2. _____   _____   _____

Word Chains

These chains are made just like some holiday paper-chain decorations. Cut up the strips on page 39. Write one spellling word from your word list on its center using large letters. Find a different word from your list that begins with the last letter of the first word you selected. If you can't find a list word, think of another word that would fit. Continue adding words in the same way. See how many of your spelling words you can fit into your chain. Can you use them all? Glue your chain together in order.

> If you can use at least 10 of your words, you are doing a great job. If you can use 15 words, you are a Word Wizard. If you can use 18 words, you are a Word Expert. If you use all 20 you are a Word Grand Master!

Example:

1. | fas<u>t</u> |
2. | <u>t</u>el<u>l</u> |
3. | <u>l</u>ette<u>r</u> |
4. | <u>r</u>igh<u>t</u> |
5. | <u>t</u>abl<u>e</u> |

and on and on . . .

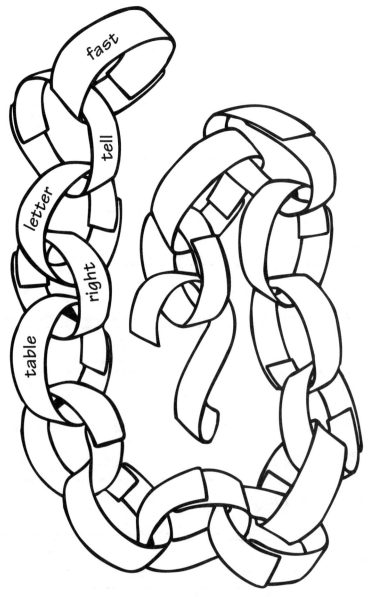

Word Chains

Cut along the dashed lines to make individual strips.

Column Spelling

Write your spelling word in column 1. Copy the word to column 2. Now fold your paper and write the word from memory in column 3. Unfold your paper and check to see if you spelled it correctly. Try again if you missed the word. Practice one word at a time.

Column 1	Column 2	Column 3
1. _____	_____	_____
2. _____	_____	_____
3. _____	_____	_____
4. _____	_____	_____
5. _____	_____	_____
6. _____	_____	_____
7. _____	_____	_____
8. _____	_____	_____
9. _____	_____	_____
10. _____	_____	_____
11. _____	_____	_____
12. _____	_____	_____
13. _____	_____	_____
14. _____	_____	_____
15. _____	_____	_____
16. _____	_____	_____
17. _____	_____	_____
18. _____	_____	_____
19. _____	_____	_____
20. _____	_____	_____

Bonus Word(s):

1. _____ _____ _____

2. _____ _____ _____

Guide Words

Look up your words in a dictionary. Write down the two guide words you find on the top of the dictionary pages. The guide words tell you the first and last word found on that page.

Word	Guide Words
1. _____	_____
2. _____	_____
3. _____	_____
4. _____	_____
5. _____	_____
6. _____	_____
7. _____	_____
8. _____	_____
9. _____	_____
10. _____	_____
11. _____	_____
12. _____	_____
13. _____	_____
14. _____	_____
15. _____	_____
16. _____	_____
17. _____	_____
18. _____	_____
19. _____	_____
20. _____	_____

Bonus Word(s):

1. _____ _____

2. _____ _____

Three Times in Color

Write each word three times using a different color each time.

1. _____ _____ _____

2. _____ _____ _____

3. _____ _____ _____

4. _____ _____ _____

5. _____ _____ _____

6. _____ _____ _____

7. _____ _____ _____

8. _____ _____ _____

9. _____ _____ _____

10. _____ _____ _____

11. _____ _____ _____

12. _____ _____ _____

13. _____ _____ _____

14. _____ _____ _____

15. _____ _____ _____

16. _____ _____ _____

17. _____ _____ _____

18. _____ _____ _____

19. _____ _____ _____

20. _____ _____ _____

Bonus Word(s):

1. _____ _____ _____

2. _____ _____ _____

Short Story

Write a short story on a separate sheet of paper using as many of your list words as you can. Underline the words you used and list them in the word box below. Remember, a story needs to have a beginning, middle, and end. It also needs a title, characters, and a conflict that is resolved at the end of your story.

Look at your word list and choose one that gives you an idea for a topic. For instance, if one of your spelling words is *picnic*, you might write about a picnic you have been on or a make-believe one.

Don't forget to write a rough draft and to revise and edit your story. When editing, make sure to check for paragraph structure, spelling, and punctuation. Does your story make sense when you read it back to yourself? Write your final draft neatly and attach it to this paper.

Word Box

_____ _____ _____

_____ _____ _____

_____ _____ _____

_____ _____ _____

_____ _____ _____

_____ _____ _____

Fill in the Blank

Use each of your words in a sentence. Leave the word out of your sentence (draw a line where the word should go). Give it to a friend to fill in the blanks. Don't forget capitals and punctuation.

1. _____

   _____

2. _____

   _____

3. _____

   _____

4. _____

   _____

5. _____

   _____

6. _____

   _____

7. _____

   _____

8. _____

   _____

9. _____

   _____

10. _____

   _____

Fill in the Blank

11. _____

12. _____

13. _____

14. _____

15. _____

16. _____

17. _____

18. _____

19. _____

20. _____

Bonus Word(s):

1. _____

2. _____

Crossword Puzzle

Using the blank grid below, plan a crossword puzzle that contains at least 10 of your words. Each word and its clue are numbered with the same number. The words cross each other and share one letter (see example below). Once you have your puzzle planned, list the words and the numbered clues on the puzzle page (page 47). On the grid will be just the numbers with the correct amount of squares for each word. For example, the word *fit* takes 3 squares, *firm* takes 4. Draw a box around the squares and number them. Check your grid below to guide you. Check your contract for specific activity instructions.

Example

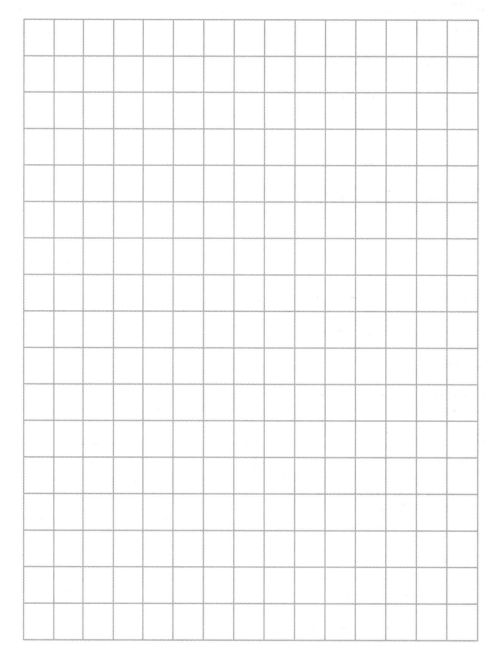

Clues

Across

2. strong

3. to be

Down

1. solid

Crossword Puzzle

Words

_____ _____ _____

_____ _____ _____

_____ _____ _____

_____ _____ _____

Clues

Across

_____

_____

_____

_____

_____

_____

_____

Down

_____

_____

_____

_____

_____

_____

_____

Word Sort

Sort your spelling words into categories of your own choosing. Write the category names at the top of each column.

CATEGORY 1	CATEGORY 2	CATEGORY 3

Alliteration

Write your list words in sentences using alliteration. *Alliteration* is when words beginning with the same consonant sound are used throughout a sentence.

Example: <u>W</u>e <u>w</u>ent <u>w</u>alking <u>w</u>ith <u>W</u>endy on <u>W</u>ednesday.

1. _____
2. _____
3. _____
4. _____
5. _____
6. _____
7. _____
8. _____
9. _____
10. _____
11. _____
12. _____
13. _____
14. _____
15. _____
16. _____
17. _____
18. _____
19. _____
20. _____

Bonus Word(s):

1. _____
2. _____

Dictionary Definitions

Look up your words in a dictionary and write the definitions.

Words

1. _____
2. _____
3. _____
4. _____
5. _____
6. _____
7. _____
8. _____
9. _____
10. _____

Definitions

1. _____
   _____
2. _____
   _____
3. _____
   _____
4. _____
   _____
5. _____
   _____
6. _____
   _____
7. _____
   _____
8. _____
   _____
9. _____
   _____
10. _____
    _____

Dictionary Definitions

Words	Definitions
11. _____	**11.** _____
12. _____	**12.** _____
13. _____	**13.** _____
14. _____	**14.** _____
15. _____	**15.** _____
16. _____	**16.** _____
17. _____	**17.** _____
18. _____	**18.** _____
19. _____	**19.** _____
20. _____	**20.** _____

Bonus Word(s):

1. _____	**1.** _____
2. _____	**2.** _____

Word Match

In column A, write 10 words from your list that you are having the most problem learning. Next, look them up in a dictionary and write the definitions in column B. Be sure to mix up the definitions by writing them on a different line than the list word. Then, give it to a friend and have him or her draw lines to match the words in column A to their definitions in column B. Check their work. How did they do?

Column A   **Column B**

1. _____   • _____
                                                          _____

2. _____   • _____
                                                          _____

3. _____   • _____
                                                          _____

4. _____   • _____
                                                          _____

5. _____   • _____
                                                          _____

6. _____   • _____
                                                          _____

7. _____   • _____
                                                          _____

8. _____   • _____
                                                          _____

9. _____   • _____
                                                          _____

10. _____   • _____
                                                          _____

Who Did What?

Instructions

1. On a set of 10 cards, write the name or job title of a person, or write a type of animal (one per card). Cut out the cards provided on page 55 or use index cards.

2. On a second set of 10 cards, write an action word with the suffix *–ed* added (include any of your list words that are verbs).

3. On a third set of 10 cards, write a word that names a thing (include any of your list words that are nouns).

4. Keep the cards in three separate piles.

5. Pick one card from each pile. Now make a sentence with those three words, adding other words so that it makes sense. The sentences can be silly. See example below.

6. Write your sentences on page 54. Don't forget capitals and correct punctuation.

7. Underline the three original words in each sentence.

8. Continue until you have used all of your cards and have 10 complete sentences written.

Example

| farmer | shouted | bookcase |

The <u>farmer</u> was so angry when the horse knocked down his <u>bookcase</u>, that he <u>shouted</u> for ten minutes.

Who Did What?

Sentences

1. _____
   _____

2. _____
   _____

3. _____
   _____

4. _____
   _____

5. _____
   _____

6. _____
   _____

7. _____
   _____

8. _____
   _____

9. _____
   _____

10. _____
    _____

Who Did What?

Cut apart the rectangles below to use as cards or use index cards.

Prefix/Suffix

In column A, write the base or root word. In column B, write the prefix or suffix. In column C, write how the word part changed the meaning of your root or base word.

	Column A	**Column B**	**Column C**
1.	_____	_____	_____
2.	_____	_____	_____
3.	_____	_____	_____
4.	_____	_____	_____
5.	_____	_____	_____
6.	_____	_____	_____
7.	_____	_____	_____
8.	_____	_____	_____
9.	_____	_____	_____
10.	_____	_____	_____
11.	_____	_____	_____
12.	_____	_____	_____
13.	_____	_____	_____
14.	_____	_____	_____
15.	_____	_____	_____
16.	_____	_____	_____
17.	_____	_____	_____
18.	_____	_____	_____
19.	_____	_____	_____
20.	_____	_____	_____

Bonus Word(s):

1.	_____	_____	_____
2.	_____	_____	_____

Contraction Parts

Write your contraction in the first column and write the two words that make up your contraction in the second. Then write the letters that were left out of your contraction in the third column.

Contraction	Two Words	Missing Letters
1. _____	_____	_____
2. _____	_____	_____
3. _____	_____	_____
4. _____	_____	_____
5. _____	_____	_____
6. _____	_____	_____
7. _____	_____	_____
8. _____	_____	_____
9. _____	_____	_____
10. _____	_____	_____
11. _____	_____	_____
12. _____	_____	_____
13. _____	_____	_____
14. _____	_____	_____
15. _____	_____	_____
16. _____	_____	_____
17. _____	_____	_____
18. _____	_____	_____
19. _____	_____	_____
20. _____	_____	_____

Bonus Word(s):

1. _____ _____ _____

2. _____ _____ _____

Contraction List

Make a list of as many contractions as you can find. Write the contraction and the two words that make it up on each line. **Example**: don't/do not

_____	_____	_____
_____	_____	_____
_____	_____	_____
_____	_____	_____
_____	_____	_____
_____	_____	_____
_____	_____	_____
_____	_____	_____
_____	_____	_____
_____	_____	_____
_____	_____	_____
_____	_____	_____
_____	_____	_____
_____	_____	_____
_____	_____	_____
_____	_____	_____
_____	_____	_____
_____	_____	_____
_____	_____	_____
_____	_____	_____
_____	_____	_____
_____	_____	_____
_____	_____	_____

Blank Homophone Sentences

Write a sentence using both of your homophones in context. Leave a blank line where the homophones should go. Write the homophone pair at the end of the sentence in parentheses. Then switch papers with a classmate and complete each other's sentences.

Example: She bought the new _____ for one _____. (scent, cent)

1. _____

   _____

2. _____

   _____

3. _____

   _____

4. _____

   _____

5. _____

   _____

6. _____

   _____

7. _____

   _____

8. _____

   _____

9. _____

   _____

10. _____

   _____

Blank Homophone Sentences

11. _____

_____

12. _____

_____

13. _____

_____

14. _____

_____

15. _____

_____

16. _____

_____

17. _____

_____

18. _____

_____

19. _____

_____

20. _____

_____

Bonus Word(s):

1. _____

_____

2. _____

_____

Homophone Sentences

Write a sentence using both of your homophones in context.

Example: She bought the new scent for one cent.

1. _____

   _____

2. _____

   _____

3. _____

   _____

4. _____

   _____

5. _____

   _____

6. _____

   _____

7. _____

   _____

8. _____

   _____

9. _____

   _____

10. _____

    _____

Homophone Sentences

11. _____

    _____

12. _____

    _____

13. _____

    _____

14. _____

    _____

15. _____

    _____

16. _____

    _____

17. _____

    _____

18. _____

    _____

19. _____

    _____

20. _____

    _____

Bonus Word(s):

1. _____

   _____

2. _____

   _____

Homophones List

Make a list of as many homophone pairs as you can find.

_____ , _____   _____ , _____

_____ , _____   _____ , _____

_____ , _____   _____ , _____

_____ , _____   _____ , _____

_____ , _____   _____ , _____

_____ , _____   _____ , _____

_____ , _____   _____ , _____

_____ , _____   _____ , _____

_____ , _____   _____ , _____

_____ , _____   _____ , _____

_____ , _____   _____ , _____

_____ , _____   _____ , _____

_____ , _____   _____ , _____

_____ , _____   _____ , _____

_____ , _____   _____ , _____

_____ , _____   _____ , _____

_____ , _____   _____ , _____

_____ , _____   _____ , _____

Singulars and Plurals

Write your list of plurals in the first column and write the singular form of each word in the second column.

Plurals	Singulars
1. _____	_____
2. _____	_____
3. _____	_____
4. _____	_____
5. _____	_____
6. _____	_____
7. _____	_____
8. _____	_____
9. _____	_____
10. _____	_____
11. _____	_____
12. _____	_____
13. _____	_____
14. _____	_____
15. _____	_____
16. _____	_____
17. _____	_____
18. _____	_____
19. _____	_____
20. _____	_____

Bonus Word(s):

1. _____ _____

2. _____ _____